"The best and most beautiful things in the world can not be seen or even touched; they must be felt with the heart."
~ Helen Keller

Poems at Last
For Hearts of Glass

By : Michael Kent Taylor

iUniverse, Inc.
New York   Bloomington

Poems at Last for Hearts of Glass

Copyright © 2009 Michael Kent Taylor

iUniverse books may be ordered through booksellers or by contacting:

iUniverse
1663 Liberty Drive
Bloomington, IN 47403
www.iuniverse.com
1-800-Authors (1-800-288-4677)

ISBN: 978-1-4401-1475-5 (pbk)
ISBN: 978-1-4401-1476-2 (ebk)

Library of Congress Control Number: 2009920324

Printed in the United States of America

iUniverse rev. date: 1/15/2009

Contents

Hearts of Glass	1
A Fire Fly's Dance	2
What a Shame	3
The Kiss	4
Time and Space	5
Internet Love	6
A Lovers Dance	7
Fun in the Sun	8
Stolen Fun	9
Just One Kiss	10
Melted Ice Cream	11
Strangers Meet	12
Sweet Radiance	13
Beach's Shore	14
Eye's of my Heart	15
Man's Reflection	16
Mirror's of my Mind	17
A Foggy Winter Kiss	18
Under the Moon	19
A Love Most Unkind	20
A Rose	21
One More Tear	22
Tattered Rag	23
A Lost Shoe	24
Candy Shop	25
Victoria's Bra	26
Season's Change	27
Fly Away	28
The Rapture	29
Leave's Romance	30

Starry Night	31
Red, Yellow and Gold	32
Floating	33
The Red Rose	34
Reflections Back	35
The Tost	36
The Gloom	37
God's Grace	38
Spider's Web	39
What the Shell's do Tell	40
Love's Last Embrace	41
A Drift	42
Call of the Leave's	43
A Bitch	44
Words of Fire	45
Angel of Night	46
Unicorn	47
Name	48
The Shadow	49
Winters Heart	50
The Rain	51
Morning Light	52
The Beacon	53
Thanks to Tiffany's	54
The End	55

Poems at Last for Hearts of Glass

Goes out to all those hearts that have been chipped, cracked, broken or shattered.

To all those hearts of glass its time at last to put it all in the past.

Michael Kent Taylor, Author

Please visit my web site at: TaylorMichaelk.com

This book of poetry is filled with different feelings and emotions. After going through a very difficult break up with someone I loved very much. I felt that there was nothing left to live for. I became very sick and began to drink and smoke. I hit rock bottom when I ended up in the hospital the day after Christmas 2005. I had lost a lot of weight and in so doing so weakened my immune system. I was so weak and sick that I lost part of my vision which I will never get back. It was then that I decided that enough was enough and I had to do something so I began to write. At first it was a diary then more like a memoir. But then I started to write poetry and the stuff just came out. So I wrote this book for all those people who have been where I have been. They wear their hearts on their sleeves and end up hurt, lost and confused, asking what did I do. Well let me tell you first IT's NOT YOUR FAULT!! The problem is theirs not with you. So by writing this book of poems I hope in some small way I can give someone hope or at least something that will help. My goal is not to become famous or make money but to let others know there are people out there that care and have been to hell and back. I don't offer advice but my Grandfather Peterson once told me "You can always tell a persons character by the way they walk and talk. If they talk and their upper lip don't move then don't trust them. If they walk and you can't hear their steps then they're kind of heart. But if they sound like an elephant then they will stomp all over it." So I guess my advice, if I was asked would be, BEWARE THE ELEPHANTS. As for me well I'm 39 single and live in Richmond Virginia with my two children (my dogs, grand dogs to my mother) Tigger and Pooka. We have been here for the past 10 yrs. They go every where with me. I grew up in Battleboro North Carolina. It's a small farming town in North Eastern North Carolina. One of those towns where everyone new each other and you didn't have to lock your doors at night. My parents divorced when I was 6 however I was blessed with the worlds best Mom and Dad. Anyone can father a child but it takes a special man to be a Dad. They raised me well and I thank them for making me do all the things I hated to do as a child. You know making up your bed each morning, pulling grass from the garden, cutting the grass, Daddy even made me work on my car. He use to make me go and cut wood in the mornings in the winter till I was 14. Then he told me I had a choice either cut wood with him or get a work permit and go to work. Well I chose the work permit and started working at 14 and have been working ever since. My Mom taught me to clean, cook, wash and iron clothes. I tell you I can cook a mean pot of collards. I went to school at Rocky Mount Academy then Northern Nash Senior High after graduation I attended East Carolina University. I am currently a member of The Poetry Society of America and The Poetry Society of Virginia. I love to read and have been all over the US , London and Paris. I love to travel, read, workout, go hiking, wine tastings, and all kinds of music and movies. I hope everyone enjoys the book and look for my second book <u>Somewhere Between Day and Night</u> coming out soon. Please feel free to contact me at TaylorMichaelK@Aol.com or visit my web site at TaylorMichaelK.com. I really hope you enjoy the book as much as I did in writing it. ~Michael Kent

Pooka

Mom and Dad

Tigger

Hearts of Glass

Here I stand alone at last

All alone with my heart of glass

Our time together went so fast

My heart was shattered way to fast

Now my shadow has been cast

My heart and soul have gone at last

In a shadow on the floor

And from that shadow on the floor

My heart and soul will rise no more

For our time has come to past

Some say true love never lasts

When you have a Heart of Glass

A Fire Fly's Dance

Watch the fire flies as they twinkle

See them dance like stars that twinkle

For as long as fire flies fly and stars twinkle

They make me think of warm summer nights gone in
a twinkle

For nothing gives my eye a little twinkle

Than when I remember the fire flies and how they
twinkled

What a Shame

You called my name

Oh what a shame

I felt the flame

Oh what pain

It felt like rain

What a Shame

Your touch hot like a flame

I burned with desire

Just a kiss and my souls on fire

It felt so very nice

Then like the cold of ice

You called my name

Then you left me in the rain

Wet and cold with my pain

The Kiss

Like Fire and Ice

You felt so nice

My soul on fire

You made me go higher and higher

Each Kiss you set my heart on fire

With each desire I called your name

My heart was still a flame

But then you left me in the rain

Leaving me all alone with my pain

Time and Space

In both Time and Space

We held our place

I saw your sweet face

My heart began to race

What a shame you could not keep the pace

For we had a love

Both in Time and Space

Internet Love

We meet on line

That was fine

And for a time

You were mine

And for that time

While you were mine

You and I lost our prime

You moved on in that time

While I stood lost in mine

All alone with a ghost

Lost in time as do most

But here I stand alone at last

In a home with nothing more

Than a ghost without a host

A Lovers Dance

Lovers prance

A passionate dance

At long last

Its come to past

Time has gone all to fast

For this passionate dance

Now it's time to end at last

Our one true chance

To see our lovers one last Dance

Fun in the Sun

Here at last we had our fun

We had our time in the sun

And from this fun we had in the sun

The time has gone and so has the sun

What's been done can't be undone

For our time of fun in the sun

Is a time that we had not begun

So enjoy the sun and the fun

For time will come all to fast

Then it will be a memory forever lost in the past.

Stolen Fun

At last it's come

Our fun is done

No more fun in the sun

The time has come

And stolen our fun

There's no more fun in the sun

For time has undone all that was fun

Just One Kiss

Oh sweet kiss

The one that I miss

You placed my heart in rapture

My heart and soul you did capture

With just one kiss I was in rapture

And in that one kiss you did capture

The monster known only unto me

For my heart and soul you had captured

And in the rapture my heart and soul you did destroy

All of which you had captured

With just a kiss you did destroy

All of which you'd held in rapture

Melted Ice Cream

I once had dreams

One's of fields and of streams

And in those dreams we'd run through fields and fish
in streams

We'd yell and scream and run for ice cream

I sit here now 30 dreams past

I listen for the sound of time long past

I remember when I use to dream of summers past

I remember now my childhood dreams

Dreams of fields and streams and melted ice cream

Strangers Meet

It doesn't take much with words of sweet deceit

We meet as strangers on the street

But oh how sweet when as friends we do meet

Then with words of deceit we become lovers as we sleep

But oh how sweet the deceit when at first we did meet

For lovers under the sheets whispers nothing of deceit

But it doesn't take much with words of sweet deceit

For lovers to deceive and leave with words of deceit

Whispered under the sheets

Sweet Radiance

Oh time how you are sweet

But with the sweet comes a face most devious

For time is oblivious of such deviance

But then in sweet light your face reflects a light of
such radiance

And from that light that radiates out

Comes a heart we can't do without

For time doesn't hold still for faces that pout

And hearts don't do without

Faces that are oblivious to hearts that doubt

Beach's Shore

See the moon dance along the beaches shore

Watch it dance along the beach's shore

See how it looks and adores the shore

And as we dance and adore the beaches shore

We search no more for lovers that we adore

For nothing matters more

Than the moon that dances on the shore

And nothing more do we adore

Than lovers that we search for no more

Eye's of my Heart

Let me show you the world through my eyes

For my eyes will tell you no lies

Through my eyes you will see where my true love lies

For without true love you could not see

Through my eyes to the heart that tells no lies

Man's Reflection

Man melts sand to see the world outside

He melts colors to project the light from inside

And from that light projected through the sand

That he melted with his own hands

Man can see his own reflection sitting by his side

A moving picture that reflects the life from inside

A life which he cannot hide

Mirror's of my Mind

As I look into the mirrors of my mind

I wish I could stop time and just re-wind

Ah but at last how time comes to past

And how the mirrors never last

Oh how I wish in my mind

I could find the time

To just sit and have my mind re-wind time

A Foggy Winter Kiss

See the foggy mist as it creeps into winter's bliss

Look for its warm and longing kiss

For winters time has yet to come

At least not in all its bliss

It seems to long for the fall that it missed

Now give us peace for this bliss

That we have missed

For nothing last like winters foggy kiss

Under the Moon

I feel your lips on my finger tips

I hear your sweet words leave your lips

I wait for the night so I can hold you tight

In moons light I feel the time is right

I reach for you and find only night

Was the time not right

Was my lover not ready for the light

I fear love is not worth the fight

I leave like a thief in the night

Without the delight of holding my lover tight

Under the sweet moon light

A Love Most Unkind

Love can be gentle love can be unkind

I do not need to sleep to find you in my time

For love can't be mine at least not in my time

So I move through space and time

I try to find the love that must be mine

But love is most unkind

I still search for love to be mine

But I know it want be in my time

So I leave it all behind to move forward in time

For love has been most unkind

A Rose

I wake and feel like a newborn

In your arms I am adorn

All my fears I have no more

For here I lie forever more

For you adorn me no more

For you have left a rose with a thorn

A lover scorned and nothing more

One More Tear

I do not shed a single tear

For the things that I hold most dear

Through time and space I cannot fear

For the thing I hold most dear

Love has never been mine that is clear

My heart and love is what I held dear

This I will not fear nor shed a single tear

For in my heart I hold no fear nor nothing dear

For in my heart my lover shall not be near

And I fear that I shall shed just one more tear

Tattered Rag

The sky above me has turned grey

I'm afraid my heart and soul have been led astray

My life like an old tattered rag has begun to fray

I have no strength and cannot stay

The time has come at last for me to leave and lay

So in the fields a bed I make in the hay

I'm looking above into the sky that is grey

Thinking of the love that led me astray

I cannot stay for night has come my way

Now forever I must lay

Under starry sky that's turned grey

My heart and soul thrown away like an old rag tattered and frayed

A Lost Shoe

Wondering through life will love come home to you

Love should be gentle, kind but true

But will love come home to you

For sometimes love is like a lost shoe

But if given time it will come home to you

So look no more for the shoe

Nor for the love that is true

For if it was yours it will come home to you

Candy Shop

Come and take me to your candy shop

We can stop and find our sweet spot

I can feel it's getting hot

So take me to the candy shop

We can't stop since it's so hot

Come and give me what you got

It want take a lot

So come take me to your sweet spot

I can't wait take me to your candy shop

Now hurry lover for I'm about to pop

For love can't be stopped while you're in the candy
shop

Victoria's Bra

Faster faster please give me a thrill

I find I have no need for a pill

I've gone to the mall

In search of it all

I found a candelabra

And Victoria's bra

Now faster faster give me a thrill

It's to late my drink I did spill

I found out I had no use for a pill

So faster faster give me a thrill

For I have lost sense of all that is real

Season's Change

Fall has come

Summer is done

We had our fun

Now winters come

Our time has past

We have learned at last

It's all gone to fast

The shadow has been cast

We can't get past

That which lies

Both in space and in time

Here we see the face

But we lack the pace

To keep up with both time and space

So let go this face

And remain in place

For time holds no space

For a loves lost face

Fly Away

Tonight I laid my eyes on you

I looked through yours and saw only you

I got nervous when you looked my way

But you knew all the words to say

That made me feel this way

You knew just what to say

That would take my breath away

Your kiss made me sway

With each breath you led me astray

Now I have to stay

My heart you led away

No more kiss to make me sway

No more looks to make me lay

Please just let me slip away

For love has led me all this way

No more time to stay and play

Just the time to fly away

The Rapture

With our love in rapture

My heart and soul you did capture

I looked into your eyes and saw our future

My heart and soul you had captured

Now our future has come and gone

And you have moved on

You left my heart fractured

Our love that you captured

Has now left us fractured

I fear I have no future

For our love is not in rapture

Leave's Romance

See the leaves dance to summers romance

See how they keep time to its dance

Now fall has come the romance must change

See the colored leaves as they change

Both in color and in time

For now winter has found its time

The leaves have long been done

The green has gone

The snow has begun

Soon spring will come

And once again all will be done

The leaves of summers past

They will come at last

And once again start their summer romance

Starry Night

Look into the starry night

See the moon shining bright

My soul has been set a flight

My heart at last no longer fights

For by the moons bright light

I find the strength to fight

To set my heart and soul to flight

On moon beams so bright

I reach a new height

And see with new sight

At long last I hold tight

For at last I do not fight

For my heart and soul I have set to flight

Red, Yellow and Gold

See the leaves of red, yellow and of gold

Watch them twist and turn and do as they're told

They turn and churn then bend and fold

For they know they can no longer hold

The wind has blown and they've been told

Let go and fold you're leaves of red, yellow and gold

For winters come and placed you on hold

And as the snow does fall

So must the leaves of red, yellow and gold

Floating

My heart and soul float down a stream

My thoughts and dreams clouded as if by cream

I feel as though I may scream

My life was full of dreams

Now all my hopes and dreams float down a stream

So if I had my life to live over I am sure I would not
dream

For I have learned all they do is make me scream

The Red Rose

A red rose do I hold

My heart and soul I have sold

And through my rose my hearts been told

Your soul I'm sorry I cannot hold

For a lie they've been told

My heart shouts to my rose that I hold

Why poor rose were you told

My soul you could not hold

Oh my rose I should tell

For all my lovers they have fell

And now they all live in hell

Reflections Back

Like a rose all my lovers they had thorns

How many thorns can a rose have you may ask

How many thorns can a lover lack

My thoughts they do reflect back

Three I can count of which I did lack

For I do lack the nack to get love back

For my lovers all lied in the sack

And now I don't want them back

The Tost

Let us have a drink

To all those lovers whom we think

For my heart they do stink

For mine they played tricks

So I just sit here and think

And say to you that do drink

Don't think of love that stinks

Just let love pass and think

For lovers they turn tricks

And say words that play tricks

Then makes our heart sick

So let love be since it stinks

Sit and have just a drink

For words do trick

But love still stinks

The Gloom

There I was full of gloom

Sitting all alone in my room

I found myself thinking of you

Then you came like a feathered plume

You came dancing across the room

I felt my heart as it bloomed

Then I knew I'd been fooled

For it was you I needed to chase away the gloom

God's Grace

God in Heaven lend me grace

For I have not a beautiful face

For love is lost both in time and in space

I wish to go to the place

Where in God's hands I can place

My faith that love will come back

To me both in time and in space

Till that time my faith I will keep

Until God's grace I shall sleep

Spider's Web

As I lay in my bed

A spider's web I did see

And laying in that web that I see

A heart of mine that's been left to dangle

Oh but what a web my heart was tangled

For like a fly left to dangle

My heart was left to strangle

Now I lay in my bed nothing more do I see

Except for my spider that I see

For it's my heart that he see's

Now he tangles and he strangles

All that love has entangled

What the Shell's do Tell

Come and walk along the beach

Watch the waves and see them reach

For the sand along the beach

It is time for them to teach

And so we listen to their speech

It's the shells that do preach

So listen closely as they teach

For they speak of love that's been breached

So I sit on sandy beach

And I listen to the shells

And all they do tell

For love is hell from what they tell

So listen to me and do not fail

For it's the story of the shells that I tell

Love's Last Embrace

Come and listen to my tail

Of love and lovers as they sail

Through time and space their hearts raced

And in time their hearts we embraced

For nothing more could they face

Than the thought of loves last embrace

So come with me and listen to the shells

And all they have to tell

Of love that's gone all to hell

A Drift

Watch the smoke as it drifts

Set adrift on a lovers kiss

Now see the fire as it goes higher

See the smoke drift higher and higher

For the smoke and the fire

A heart and soul it set on fire

See the heart go higher and higher

With a soul that's on fire

For nothing more can go higher

Than a lovers soul set on fire

Call of the Leave's

Watch the leaves as they fall

Through the tree's oh so tall

And the leaves they do call

To the wind as they fall

For time is not lost no not at all

We had our time they do call

Now with the wind we must fall

A Bitch

Life's a bitch

The wind did twitch

But our hearts and souls did not switch

For our hearts and souls they do twitch

For truth be told life's a bitch

Words of Fire

Those who are liars

With words of fire

Send our hearts higher

With words that make them liars

So beware those who speak words of fire

And promises of hearts that will go higher

For just like words of fire

Those who speak them are sure to be liars

Angel of Night

Come to me my angel of the night

Take flight before the rise of sun light

Come to me in the sweet dark night

Cover me with wings of such delite

Come to me and destroy this awful light

Fly away with me into this dark night

For I fear I have lost my fight

With all that is right

My soul I've sit a flight

Come my dark knight for I will not fight

Come to night so we can take flight

Into the sweet dark starry night

Unicorn

Oh Unicorn

Oh Unicorn

You have but one horn

Your heart has no thorns

Yet you stand before me all alone

Oh but here is a rose

A rose with no horn

It to stands alone

For it has a heart surrounded by thorns

So we stand together all alone

A rose with a thorn and a Unicorn with a horn

Name

Call out my name

I did proclaim

For what's in a name

Nothing I proclaimed

For just like a flame

My heart was the same

I was so full of shame

There was no one to blame

No one with a name

No heart to set a flame

The Shadow

I have a shadow that lies on the floor

It lies and waits for a door

I'm sorry to say but there's nothing more

For the shadow on the floor

Cannot see the door

For the shadow on the floor

Has no soul to adore

So as it waits for that door

Its soul it lies upon the floor

And from that shadow on the floor

Its heart and soul will rise no more

Winters Heart

Winters here it finally came

And brought with it a chilling rain

For it's a shame for all its rain

It did not bring an end to all my pain

And then it came just like the rain

The first white snow it did fell

And here in the snow frozen like hell

Is a heart that's fell all to hell

Now hold this empty shell up to your ear

And just maybe you will hear

All that I held dear

And all that I feared

For nothing do I fear more

Than to hear my heart beat never more

The Rain

Look and see what's been born into the rain

For time and space bare no shame

Nor do they share the blame

For look what's been born from the rain

A heart and soul that share no pain

Oh but look into the eye's of the rain

For there you will see all that is plain

In the eye's of the heart and soul a burning flame

A flame that burns with no one to blame

A flame in the rain that bares no shame

For soon that flame will feel no pain

For like my hearts true pain

It will be set free in the cold dark rain

Morning Light

We meet in the warm sun light

For a time we were filled with delite

Our hearts we took to new heights

And then by cool moon light

Our hearts and souls we did unite

At first it was fright

But then it felt so right

You stayed the night

We held each other tight in each other's arms all night

At that point we knew it was right

Soon the room filled with warm sun light

By the light I saw your face my heart began to race

I knew true love had come at last

Now time has passed I know at last

I still love you both by day and by night

I'll always love you in the cool moon light

Your face a glow in the warm sunlight

The Beacon

The fog crept in as if on kitten's paws

It was thick and made the sun light pause

But then the heavens they did open

And for a while I laid there hope'n

I made a wish I would open

The door to your heart I was hope'n

For the fog can't hold back the light

And it can't hide your heart from my sight

So please don't run into the night

I hope you'll stay and fight

For its our love that will shine through the night

And the fog it will lift to show our love burning bright

Like a beacon in the night

So come and stay with me tonight

'cause soon you'll see

Our love was meant to be

Just like a beacon in the night

Thanks to Tiffany's

Come away with me to Tiffany's

We'll meet and have breakfast on our knees

We'll watch the morning as it pasts

And when the store opens up at last

We'll see all the diamonds under glass

For like the diamonds under glass

Our hearts and souls they did pass

And like the diamonds under lights

Our hearts and souls lit up the nigh

I'll never forget our moon light dance

How we looked like diamonds as we danced

Thank God for Tiffany's

For they gave us breakfast and a chance to dance

And show the world a true romance

The End

The sun has set

It's time to rest

I've done my best

I must leave and rest

Cover picture was taken by the Author at Great Falls
National Park, Virginia

This book is in loving memory of my Grandparents
Johnnie and Dell Peterson
And
Lyman and Lois Taylor I love you and miss you always
God bless and keep you till we meet again

Portions of the proceeds will be donated to HIV/AIDs
research and the ASPCA.
In honor to all those who made wrong choices while
searching for a heart that was true.
Someone that would love them and they could love
too.